Whirligigs

The Wondrous Windmills of Vollis Simpson's Imagination

Carole Boston Weatherford

Illustrated by Edwin Fotheringham

CALKINS CREEK

AN IMPRINT OF ASTRA BOOKS FOR YOUNG READERS
New York

On a North Carolina farm,
massive towers with moving parts
spin and sound in the breeze.
Did space aliens create these contraptions?

WHIRR,
CREEE'EAK.
Plink, plink.

No. Vollis Simpson did.
One of twelve children,
he was fixing things before he could read.
Even after he finished school,
he kept studying how things worked.
If you don't try something, he figured,
you don't learn anything.

Vollis aimed to make machines work better.
In the army air corps during World War II,
he got tired of doing laundry by hand.
So, he used parts from a downed B-29 bomber
to invent a wind-powered washing machine.

WHOOSH, WHOOSH, WHOOSH!

Next, he turned a bike into a motorcycle.

Vroom, Vroom,

Back home in Lucama, North Carolina, Vollis farmed and ran a machine-repair shop. To move houses, he built a huge tow truck.

Vollis made tons of machines.
To cut his family's costs on heating bills,
he made a windmill that blew
wood-heated air into their home.
Too smoky, his wife complained.

Hack, hack,
WHEEZE
Ahem, ahem.

In his sixties, Vollis got hurt and shut his shop.
The fix-it man was bored as a two-by-four.
"*I had to find something better than watching television,*" he said.

Then, a dream gave him a second wind.
With spare time, spare parts, and a heap of know-how,
Vollis hammered his vision into scrap metal.

BANG, BONK, THUD, thonk.

Using blades as propellers to capture the wind
and gears and chains to make figures move,
Vollis made a tower that turned and whizzed.

He planted his fanciful windmill on his farm.
Then, he got busy making more.
His mind was spinning.

Has Vollis gone mad? his wife wondered.
Strange hobby, the neighbors whispered.

Psst, psst, psst.
Psst, psst, psst.

Before long, tourists were stopping to stare at the quirky machines and to quiz the creator. Folks could not believe their eyes. Or ears.

Ooooh. Ahhh. Ooooh. Ahhh.

Vollis liked watching his windmills.
He built them taller and taller
until he could hardly stand them in the field.
So, he made hoists and cranes for the task.

CREEEAK, CREEEAK, grooooan.

Vollis collected junk "*too good to throw away:*"
old bikes, pipes, road signs, cotton spindles,
wheels, broken silverware, kitchen gadgets,
air conditioners, truck transmissions,
gears, ball bearings, rubber, and wood.
"*All the time . . . I was getting ideas,*" he said.
"*I was going to make something nobody ever seen.*"

Vollis made birds, dogs, horses,
airplanes, cyclists, lumberjacks,
and a guitar player inspired by his son.

N.C.

Lucama

With fan blades catching the wind,
bike wheels revolving,
mirrors and reflectors beaming,
and chimes tinkling,
Vollis's noisemaking, mechanical marvels
put little Lucama on the map.

Clink-plink-whoosh-screee!

Busloads of children visited the Windmill Farm.
Rumble, rumble, squeak, squeak.
They'd sketch the whirligigs and eat their bag lunches.
Then, Vollis would give them Blow Pops.

CRINCH,
CRUNCH,
smack,
THWOP.

After grown-up visitors begged for their own whirligigs,
Vollis made smaller ones and sold them.
Soon his windmills were turning up all over—
at the Olympics in Atlanta, and in red, white, and blue
outside the American Visionary Art Museum in Baltimore.
There, his three-ton, fifty-five-foot-tall tower
sings in the harbor breeze.

Whistle, Whir, BOING, BOING.

In time, building 'gigs took a toll on Vollis.
He got burned when a spark set his shirt on fire.
His hands were gnarled and his knees were bad.
I feel wore out, he said.
But he tinkered through the aches and pains.
Whirligigs gave him a long life, he claimed.

Time was hard on the windmills, too.
Vollis could no longer climb to care for them.
He worried that they would rust and topple over.
Luckily local leaders came to the rescue.
The town of Wilson bought thirty windmills
to restore for a park named after Vollis!

Vollis never once called himself an artist.
"*I didn't make this here to get famous,*" he said.
"*I didn't make it to get rich off it.*
I just know I wake up every day
and have to do something with my hands."

Put your hands together;
make some noise for Vollis's windmills.
His handiwork really is a sight
and a sound to behold!

"Wheels were turning in my head and I had to get them out."

Author's Note

A whirligig is a simple, often wind-powered, machine that spins or whirls and may also emit sound. When folk artist and mechanic Vollis Simpson (1919–2013) began building whirligigs at age sixty-five, the locals thought he was wacky. But his Windmill Farm in North Carolina became a roadside attraction, amusing and amazing travelers and schoolchildren alike.

After serving in World War II, Simpson ran his own machine shop on the family farm in Lucama, North Carolina. For decades, he not only repaired machines but sometimes also invented them. After an injury forced him to close his shop, dreams gave him visions of windmills. Simpson used spare parts and scrap metal to construct windmills that were both massive and elaborate. Using cranes and lifts, he stood his towers in a field on the farm.

Simpson created four whirligigs for the 1996 Olympics in Atlanta, and has pieces in the collections of the American Visionary Art Museum in Baltimore, the American Folk Art Museum in New York City, and the North Carolina Museum of Art in Raleigh. The whirligigs have been named North Carolina's official folk art.

In Wilson, North Carolina, windmills from the Simpson family farm are being restored and placed in a park named in Vollis's honor. A museum next door commemorates his life and his art.

Vollis Simpson poses at his Windmill Farm in Lucama, North Carolina.

Bold colors and whimsical scenes are hallmarks of Simpson's elaborate whirligigs.

Bibliography

The quotations used in this book can be found in the following sources marked with an asterisk (*).

Currie, Jefferson and Vollis Simpson. "Portfolio: Vollis Simpson Whirligigs." *South Writ Large*, Winter 2014. southwritlarge.com/articles/portfolio-vollis-simpson-whirligigs.

Kampe, Adam. "Vollis Simpson: Making Something Out of Nothing." *American Artscape Magazine*, National Endowment for the Arts, no. 3 (2012). arts.gov/stories/magazine/2012/3/arts-and-culture-core/vollis-simpson-making-something-out-nothing.

*Moore, Jenny. "Vollis Simpson's Whirligigs Are Moving and Not Just in the Wind!" *Folk Art Messenger*, Folk Art Society of America, 24, no. 1 (winter 2013). folkart.org/mag/vollis-simpsons-whirligigs.

National Endowment for the Arts. "Vollis Simpson: Making Something of Nothing." December 10, 2012. Video, 10:42. youtu.be/eiQTJkGFuUU.

North Carolina H.R. Res., House Resolution 1013 (2013). ncleg.net/Sessions/2013/Bills/House/HTML/H1013v2.html.

PBS NC. "Vollis Simpson Whirligig Park and Museum." *North Carolina Weekend*, October 24, 2017. Video, 4:25. youtube/q_pwO3W4xu0.

Plagens, Peter. "A Playground for Folk Art." *Wall Street Journal*, January 10, 2018. wsj.com/articles/a-playground-for-folk-art-1515617546.

Scott, Shane. "Junkyard Poet of Whirligigs and Windmills." *New York Times*, April 5, 2010. nytimes.com/2010/04/06/arts/design/06vollis.html.

*Thirteen/WNET New York. *Egg: The Arts Show*. Episode 208, "Made in the U.S.A." Aired May 17, 2001.

Vitiello, Chris. "The Extraordinary Legacy of Whirligig Creator Vollis Simpson." *INDY Week*, June 5, 2013. indyweek.com/culture/art/extraordinary-legacy-whirligig-creator-vollis-simpson.

WCNC Staff. "World-Renowned Whirligigs Go on Display in N.C." WCNC Charlotte, March 13, 2017. wcnc.com/article/news/local/world-renowned-whirligis-go-on-display-in-nc/275-422017025.

Yardley, William. "Vollis Simpson, Visionary Artist of the Junkyard, Dies at 94." *New York Times*, June 5, 2013. nytimes.com/2013/06/06/arts/design/vollis-simpson-artist-dies-at-94.html.

"Vollis Simpson's Windmill Farm"
(to the tune of "Old MacDonald Had a Farm")

Vollis Simpson had a quirk.
Me-oh-me-oh-my!
He had to know what made things work.
Me-oh-me-oh-my!

With a why, why here,
And a how, how there.
Here a how, there a why,
Everywhere a question.
Vollis Simpson had a farm.
Me-oh-me-oh-my!

Simpson's shop was on that farm.
Me-oh-me-oh-my!
Machines he fixed ran like a charm.
Me-oh-me-oh-my!

With a buzz, buzz here,
And a boing, boing there.
Here a buzz, there a boing,
Everywhere a boing, boing.
Vollis Simpson had a farm.
Me-oh-me-oh-my!

Then, one night he had a dream:
Me-oh-me-oh-my!
Towers like he'd never seen.
Me-oh-me-oh-my!

With a snore, snore here,
And a snore, snore
    there.
Here a snore, there
    a snore,
Everywhere a snore,
    snore.
Vollis Simpson had a farm.
Me-oh-me-oh-my!

Fix-It Man was thinking big,
Me-oh-me-oh-my!
Welding wondrous whirligigs.
Me-oh-me-oh-my!

With a scree, scree here,
And a scree, scree there.
Here a scree, there a scree,
Everywhere a scree, scree.
Vollis Simpson had a farm.
Me-oh-me-oh-my!

Windmills taller than the trees
    Me-oh-me-oh-my!
    Singing, spinning in the breeze.
    Me-oh-me-oh-my!

With a whir, whir here,
    And a clink, clonk there.
    Here a clink, there a clonk,
    Jingle-jangle-whoosh-bonk.
    Vollis had a windmill farm.
    Yes indeed he did!

Restored windmills
fill the sky with
sound and color
at the Vollis
Simpson Whirligig
Park in Wilson,
North Carolina.

To children of all ages whose imaginations ride the wind —*CBW*
For my family, always —*EF*

Picture Credits

Vollis Simpson Whirligig Park: Photos by Keith Barnes: 28, 32;
Photos by Duffy Healey: 29, 30–31.

Calkins Creek
An imprint of Astra Books for Young Readers,
a division of Astra Publishing House
astrapublishinghouse.com

ISBN: 978-1-6626-8041-0 (hc)
ISBN: 978-1-6626-8042-7 (eBook)
Library of Congress Control Number: 2023914263

First edition

10 9 8 7 6 5 4 3 2 1

Design by Barbara Grzeslo
The text is set in Adrianna.
The art was created digitally on
a tablet with a stylus.

In his workshop, Simpson welds a creation from salvaged junk.